THE WONDERFUL WORLD OF WORDS

12

The Admiral Goes to the Rescue

Dr Lubna Alsagoff

PhD (Stanford)

Marshall Cavendish
Children

Late one night, Admiral Adjective gets an SOS, a call for help.

The next day, the admiral meets with his sailors.

A village in the kingdom, far up in the north, has run out of food.

Other Titles in the
Wonderful World of Words (WOW) Series

The admiral needed to send them some food.

Let's send them some meat, some milk, fresh fruit, vegetables, rice and grain.

3

How long does it take to sail to that village?

With our ship, we can get there in three days.

That is not good. I don't think the meat and milk will last three days on the ship.

If we sail east of the island, we can get there in two days!

That sounds better.

And with our fastest ship, we can get there in a day!

That would indeed be best!

The admiral decided that all three ships would sail to the village.

The Falcon would carry meat and milk. It could get to the village in a day!

The Eagle would carry fresh fruit and vegetables. It could get to the village in two days.

THE FALCON

THE EAG

The Albatross would carry rice and grain. It could get to the village in three days.

7

When we use adjectives to compare, we add **er** or **est** at the end of the adjective.

Adjective	Comparative	Superlative
slow	slower	slowest
tall		tallest
	lighter	
green	greener	
		sweetest

When the adjective ends with an **e**, we add **r** and **st** instead.

Adjective	Comparative	Superlative
large	larger	largest
	braver	
		bluest
strange		

When the adjective ends with a **y**, we have to change the **y** to an **i** before adding **er** or **est**.

Adjective	Comparative	Superlative
happy	happier	happiest
	busier	
		angriest
pretty		

When the adjective is a very short word, ending with one vowel and a consonant, we need to double the last consonant.

Adjective	Comparative	Superlative
slow		
sad		saddest
wet	wetter	
hot		

When the word is very long, we use **more** and **most** in front of the adjective.

Adjective	Comparative	Superlative
difficult	more difficult	difficult
enormous	enormous	enormous
horrible	horrible	horrible
expensive	expensive	expensive

A very small number of adjectives don't have **er** or **est**. They look very different!

Adjective	Comparative	Superlative
good	better	best
bad	worse	worst
far	further / farther	furthest / farthest

The Falcon and the Eagle were ready to set sail.

The soldiers were loading the last ship. But as they carried the rice and grain up to the ship, it grew heavier and heavier.

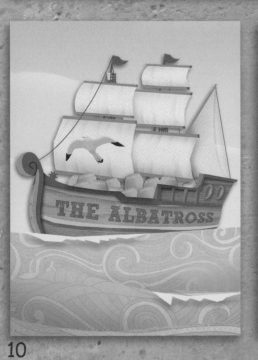

11

The admiral had to get the ship repaired. He called for the shipwright.

Make sure you use the strongest and hardest wood.

Show me the hardest and strongest wood you have!

Here it is, admiral.

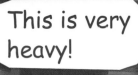

This is very heavy!

Yes, admiral, the harder the wood, the heavier it is.

This wood is too heavy! We need something lighter.

Let's use this wood. It's light, but it is stronger than other types of wood.

Perfect!

Soon, the ship was repaired, and the final ship sailed off.

THE ALBATROSS

13

Admiral Adjective was very pleased with himself. The ships had sailed, and they were on their way to help the villagers. All would be well.

So, he wrote a song. He used many wonderful adjectives to describe himself.

I'm not very t_ _l , though
I'm not all that s _ _ _ _,
but don't call me f _ _! Oh no!

I'm just rather s_ _ ut,
as an admiral should be.
My belly is _ _ u _ d,
but it's not too l_ _ _ _ .

I have the t _ _ _ k _ _ t and
b _ _ h _ _ _ _   _ _ _ _ n
moustache.

When I smile, everyone can see my
b _ _ ut _ f _ _   _ _ _ t _ teeth.

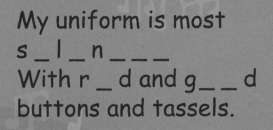

My uniform is most
s _ l _ n _ _ _
With r _ d and g _ _ d
buttons and tassels.

And a s _ _ lish hat perched on top of my head!

15

The Fabulous Forest of WOW

The animals were celebrating a very special festival. It was a festival where everyone could show off their special talents.

I am the biggest animal in the forest!
You certainly are big, Elephant! Is there anyone bigger?
No! Elephant is the biggest animal in the forest!

I am the smallest animal in the forest.
You certainly are small! Is there anyone smaller?
Hurray! Mouse is the smallest animal in the forest!

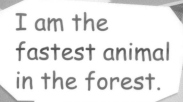

I am the fastest animal in the forest.

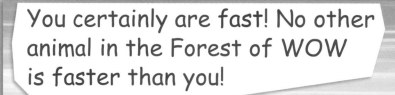

You certainly are fast! No other animal in the Forest of WOW is faster than you!

Hurray for Sloth and Tortoise!

Everyone was happy to know that Tortoise and Sloth were the slowest animals in WOW.

The animals continued to talk to each other about what they were proud of.

Monkey said he could climb the tallest tree.

And Mole told them about the deepest tunnels he had burrowed down into.

The festival ended quite suddenly when Skunk came forward.

I am the smelliest animal in the WOW Forest.

Yes, you are, Skunk! You are the smelliest in all of WOW. No animal is smellier than you!

The festival was a wonderful event. Princess Preposition could see how happy the animals were, and she was glad that the animals in WOW were so special!

23

Dear Parents,

In this issue, the children learn about how to use adjectives to make comparisons. The story introduced comparative adjectives which typically have **er** at the end, and superlative adjectives which have **est**. On pages 8 and 9, there are some useful rules that children can learn about how to make other kinds of comparatives and superlative adjectives.

Page	Possible Answers
9	slow | slowest | slowest
	tall | taller | tallest
	light | light | lightest
	sweet | sweeter | sweetest
	large | larger | largest
	brave | braver | bravest
	blue | bluer | bluest
	happy | happier | happiest
	busy | busier | busiest
	angry | angrier | angriest
	big | bigger | biggest
	sad | sadder | saddest
	wet | wetter | wettest
	difficult | more difficult | most difficult
	enormous | more enormous | most enormous
	horrible | more horrible | most horrible
14–15	tall | slim | fat
	stout | round | large
	thickest | bushiest | brown | beautiful | white
	splendid | red | gold | stylish
22	noisy – quiet
	fast – slow
	long – short
	big/large – small
	straight - curly

CERTIFICATE OF ACHIEVEMENT

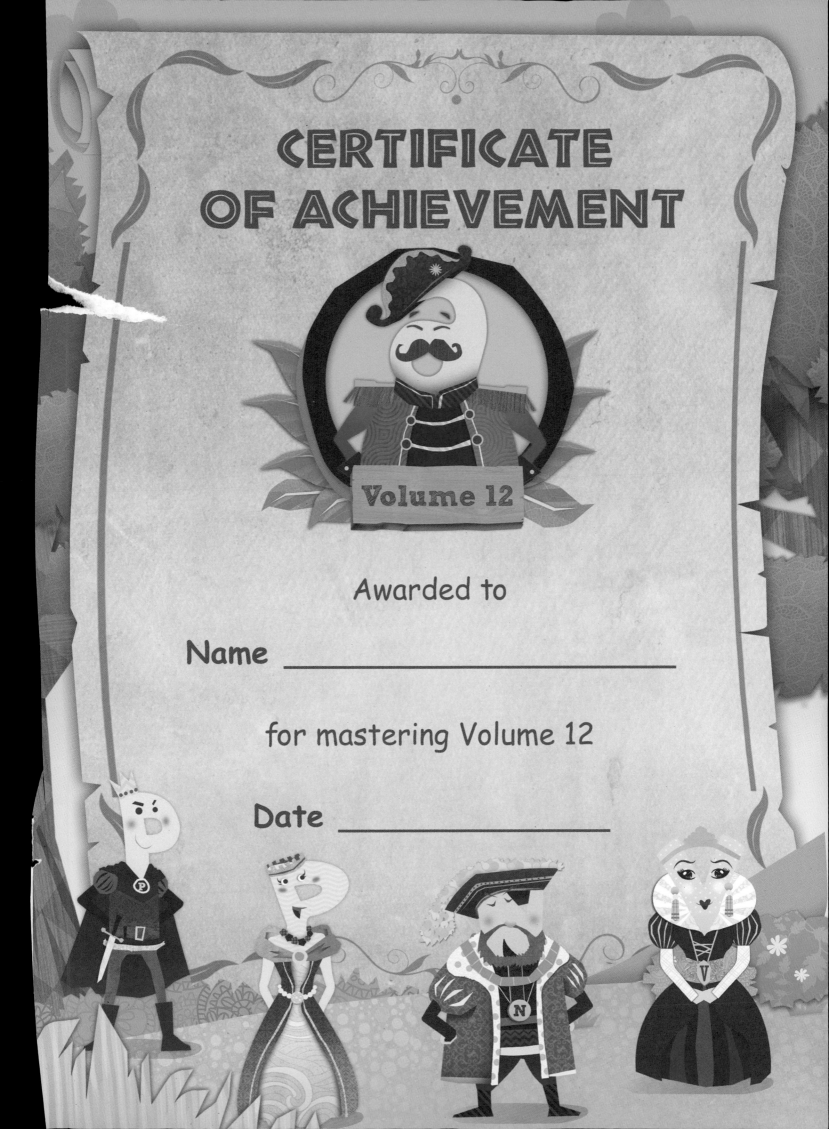

Volume 12

Awarded to

Name _____

for mastering Volume 12

Date _____

Welcome to the **Wonderful World of Words (WOW)**!

This series of books aims to help children learn English grammar in a fun and meaningful way through stories.

Children will read and discover how the people and animals of WOW learn the importance of grammar, as the adventure unfolds from volume to volume.

What's Inside

Imaginative stories that engage children, and help develop an interest in learning grammar

Adventures that encourage children to learn and understand grammar, and not just memorise rules

Games and activities to reinforce learning and check for understanding

About the Author

Dr Lubna Alsagoff is a language educator who is especially known for her work in improving the teaching of grammar in schools and in teacher education. She was Head of English Language and Literature at the National Institute of Education (NIE), and has published a number of grammar resources used by teachers and students. She has a PhD in Linguistics from Stanford University, USA, and has been teaching and researching English grammar for over 30 years.

Published by Marshall Cavendish Children
An imprint of Marshall Cavendish International

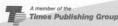
A member of the
Times Publishing Group

Printed in Singapore

visit our website at:
www.marshallcavendish.com

Marshall Cavendish
Children

CHILDREN
ISBN 978-981-5009-01-9

9 789815 009019

Some animals compared the length of their tails.

Some compared how bushy their tails were.

Can you guess which animals these belong to?
Can you write some adjectives to describe them?

1 _____ has a tail that is _____ and _____.

2 _____ has a tail that is _____ and _____.

3 _____ has a tail that is _____ and _____.

4 _____ has a tail that is _____ and _____.

5 _____ has a tail that is _____ and _____.

6 _____ has a tail that is _____ and _____.

22